Potomac Portrait

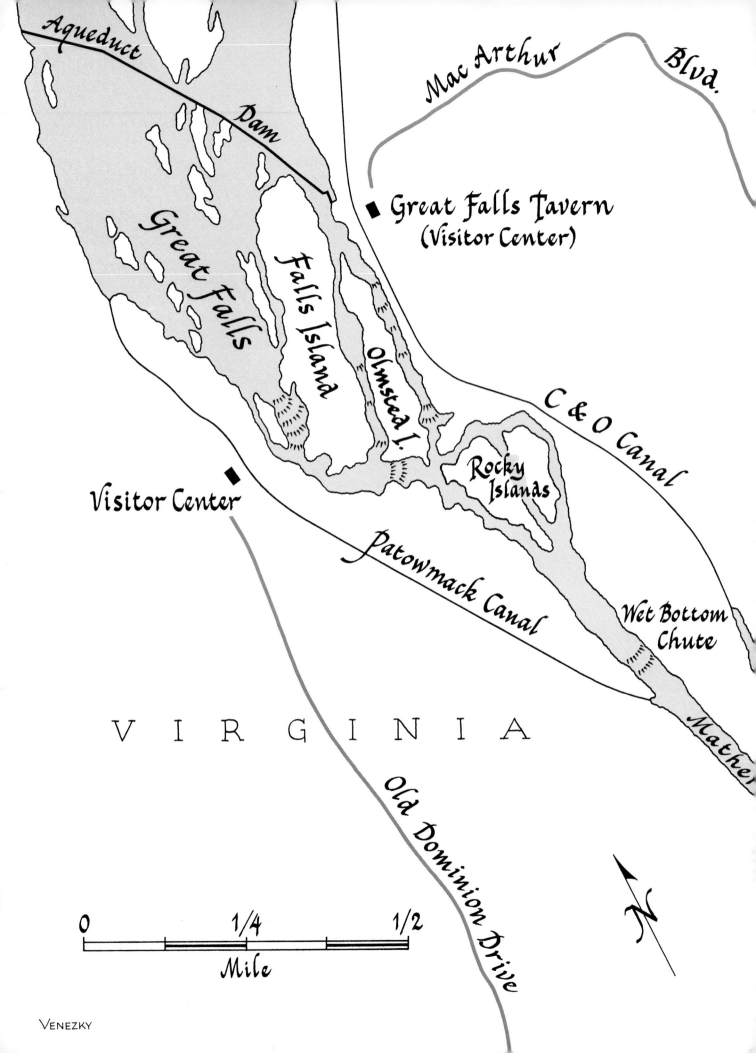

Aqueduct

Dam

Great Falls

Falls Island

Olmsted I.

■ Great Falls Tavern
(Visitor Center)

Mac Arthur Blvd.

C & O Canal

Rocky Islands

■ Visitor Center

Patowmack Canal

Wet Bottom Chute

V I R G I N I A

Mather

Old Dominion Drive

N

0   1/4   1/2
Mile

Venezky

Potomac Portrait
by
James Q. Reber

with an introduction by
William C. Everhart
National Park Service

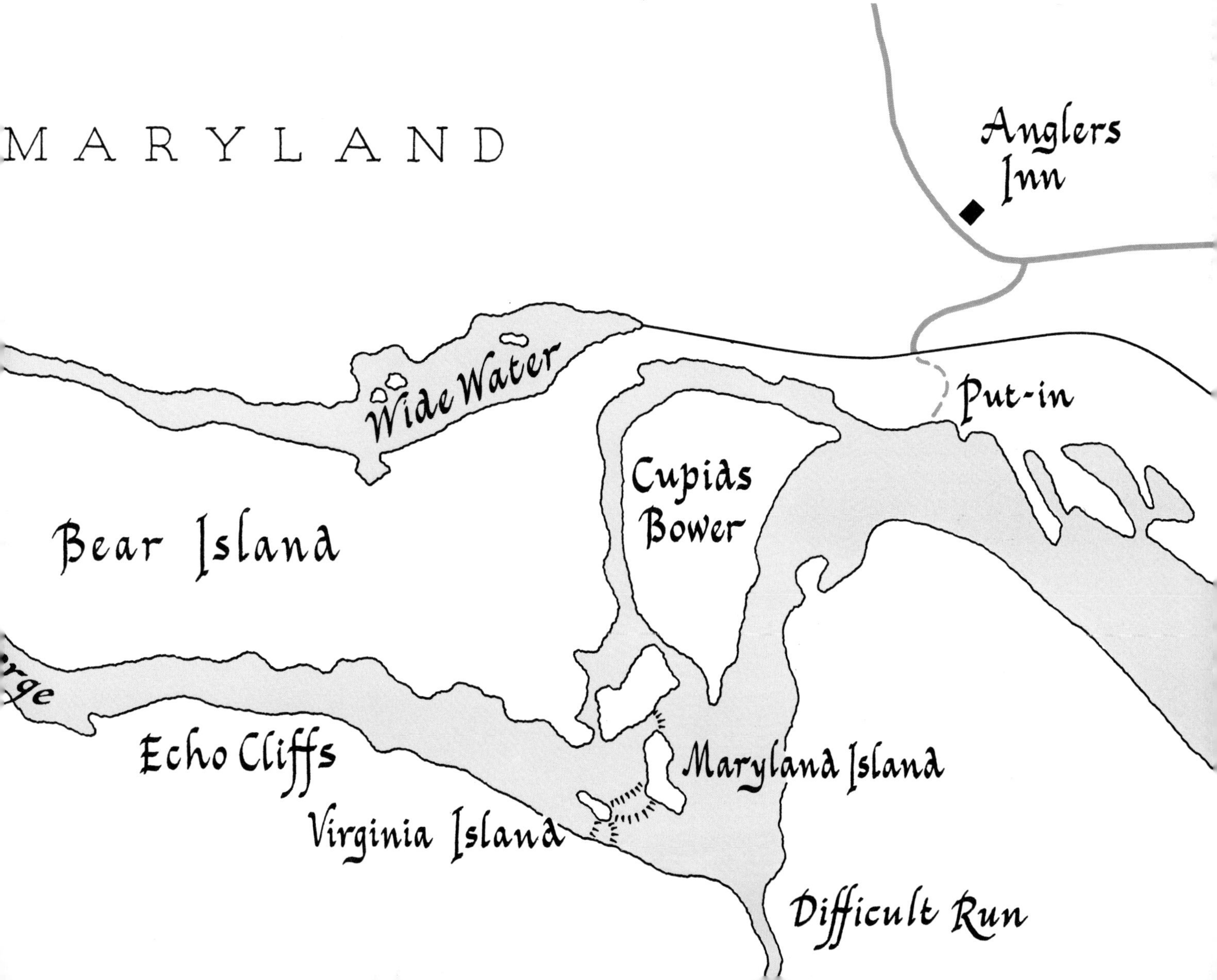

MARYLAND

Anglers
Inn

Wide Water

Put-in

Cupids
Bower

Bear Island

Echo Cliffs

Maryland Island

Virginia Island

Difficult Run

LIVERIGHT, 386 Park Avenue South
New York, New York 10016

1.987654321

ISBN: 0-87140-585-7 (cloth edition)
ISBN: 0-87140-094-4 (paper edition)
Library of Congress Catalog Card Number: 73-93128
Manufactured in the United States of America
PRINTED AND BOUND AT HALLIDAY LITHOGRAPH CORPORATION

Introduction

Some years ago, as the result of a memorable visit with Ansel Adams in his Carmel studio, I sat down with a group of National Park Service interpretive planners and suggested that we develop a national park museum whose only exhibits would be Ansel Adams photographs. The primary purpose of the museum would be to help visitors perceive the beauty of the park landscape. In my experience, most of us need this kind of assistance truly to see and appreciate the natural world around us.

The first Director of the National Park Service, Steve Mather, probably had much the same reaction, back in 1919, to an experimental program also designed to help people see.

An American traveler in one of Switzerland's mountain resorts had observed the success of a program there of conducted nature hikes. He transplanted the idea to Lake Tahoe, using trained naturalists to lay out trails and conduct evening lectures. When Mather happened by, he immediately recognized that this kind of educational program was precisely what visitors to the national parks needed to enhance their park experience. The fol-

lowing year, in 1920, he moved the program to Yosemite National Park, the beginning of interpretation in the National Park Service. Somewhere in the development of the new activity, the term "interpretation" came to replace "education," the original title. This was done, no doubt, to avoid any suggestion of the more formal classroom approach to teaching, and possibly to deter practitioners from attempting to submerge the visitor with a tide of completely accurate but exquisitely boring facts.

Interpretation also must have seemed a better term to describe the function of conveying ideas on subjects that were almost a foreign language for most people —botany, geology, or zoology. The process of translating this new language, the language of nature, suggested the term "interpretation."

Each day of the year, thousands—or more likely millions—of Americans, along with a substantial number of foreign visitors, attend interpretive programs in the national parks. Guided walks and evening campfire programs are still given. But because the number of visitors to the National Park System exceeds 200 million every year, publications, museum exhibits and films augment the work of the park interpreter. All programs seek to fulfill the goal established by Charles Darwin: "We must see with the eye of the mind." Interpretation, it has been observed, is "mindsight."

If a poet has the ability to recall for his readers a felt emotion long after the emotion has passed, a photographer has the ability to make us feel that we are really seeing a familiar scene for the first time. Jim Reber's photographs of the Potomac River landscape have this quality.

Jim came to my office a couple of years ago to show me his photographs. There is no known way to write standards for evaluating the quality of a photograph, except perhaps that the good ones always excite you. We were excited by Jim's photographs, and since that time he has carried out several photographic assignments for Park Service museums.

It is fitting that Jim's book includes coverage of the Mather Gorge of the Potomac River, named for the person who recognized the value of interpretation and launched it in the national parks more than fifty years ago. One of the goals of interpretation is not instruction, but provocation. I would hope that many readers of this book will be stimulated to take a fresh look at the Potomac River—or indeed any river or stream, or meadow or forest, nearby.

And with this deeper vision there may well come perception, which is to me the highest form of enjoyment. Our universal hope for a better environment is dependent upon our ability to perceive and treasure the natural and historic processes through which the land and all living things have achieved their form and by which they maintain their dependent existence.

We can travel to a national park only occasionally. But the grandeur of Giant Sequoias is matched by the mystery and perfection of a leaf or a river-washed stone.

WILLIAM C. EVERHART
Assistant Director, Interpretation
National Park Service

Potomac Portrait

Love of a River

My love of rivers began over fifty years ago. We lived in North Manchester, a small northern Indiana college town, on the edge of which flowed the muddy Eel River. There I learned to swim, to play underwater tag, to dive from the limb high in the elm tree by the swimming hole, and from the plank stuck in its roots. On a summer day you might have seen us cutting logs and floating them down the river for our tree house, or digging back into the riverbank for a cave hideaway.

If you're young or if you can remember your youth, you'll understand why I love a river. But the Potomac is a special river.

My love affair with the Potomac started ten years ago when I began white-water canoeing and kayaking in the area below Great Falls, a bare ten miles from the nation's capital. At first the attraction was the excitement of maneuvering in the currents and rapids. An upset in a rapids was a shocking lesson in the power of the water. Varying water levels, with consequent changes in volume, turbulence, and speed of the currents confronted the pad-dler in limitless permutations. Flood, ice, and subfreezing weather were the only hindrances to year-round paddling. At such times hikes on the trails on either side of the river gave new perspectives.

As a photographer, I could not resist the lure of Great Falls and the gorge. The river, like a lovely woman, is reluctant to reveal the secrets of her attraction to a photographer. The likeness is easy—the personality elusive. A thousand sittings for the mind's eye—with or without camera—are not enough for her portrait.

Great Falls and Mather Gorge

The section of the Potomac River from Great Falls to Little Falls at Chain Bridge on the edge of Washington, D.C., is known as the Potomac Gorge. Every part will reward the explorer. But the visual excitement of Great Falls along with the two miles below is irresistible. It includes Mather Gorge, named in honor of Stephen Mather, the father of the U.S. National Park Service.

Great Falls holds an endless fascination for me. Its limitless faces and moods may be seen by searching for vantage points, by viewing in the light of early morning and again at the end of the day, by watching for the runoff of rain and melting snow in the mountains in the spring, or the lower water levels in late summer. A snowfall is a signal to explore anew. It is not truly a falls, but a massive cataract descending some forty feet over a series of ledges. Falls Island and Olmsted Island permit intimate glimpses of cascades on a smaller scale than the main area of the falls.

The trail on either side of Mather Gorge brings a surprise at every turn. The grandeur of the area may be experienced for a pittance—a little effort, a grain of judgment, and a sure foot or paddle.

As the gorge approaches Difficult Run, the river widens. The cliffs give way to hills on the Virginia shore, and on the Maryland side Bear Island is followed by the flood plains lying below MacArthur Boulevard. The Difficult Run area with its rapids surrounding the Virginia and Maryland islands has a beauty and dignity wholly different from the falls and the gorge. In flood it becomes a vast lake whose heavy currents explode here and there in massive waves and foam. At lower water levels the modest rapids and protected coves behind the islands and rocks intrigue canoeists and kayakists. Fishermen have favorite haunts near the entry of Difficult Run and along the rocky shore upstream from the boaters' put-in below Old Angler's Inn.

Those who approach Great Falls and the gorge on the Virginia side of the river, turning off U.S. 495 on State Road 193 for

six miles to the park entrance, will find parking at the National Park Visitors Center. The center is of contemporary design, patterned after an inverted barge, similar to those used on the old Patowmack Canal, which passed through the grounds. Hikers may follow the trails downstream along Mather Gorge, past remnants of the locks of the Patowmack Canal. George Washington was a prime mover in creating the canal and was president of the enterprise from 1785 to 1789. It was a first effort to bypass Great Falls so that barges might use the river to move produce to and from the West.

The forest, second- and third-growth timber, is judged by experts to approximate its appearance in presettlement days, although there are trees growing near Difficult Run which are even more ancient. From the gorge trail the cliffs drop abruptly to the water seventy or more feet below. Along the trails one may find sandbars left by the 1972 flood caused by Hurricane Agnes. Looking upstream from the gorge to Great Falls, the line of the cliffs is straight and nearly level—evidence of the downcutting forces of erosion which produced the gorge and the falls.

On the Maryland side of the river one may reach the falls by leaving U.S. 495 at the Washington Memorial Parkway exit. The Visitors Center is located in a tavern built in 1842 beside the C and O Canal. It is a part of the C and O Canal National Historical Park which begins in Georgetown in Washington, D.C., and extends to Cumberland, Maryland. The canal parallels the Potomac, and, unlike the Patowmack Canal, uses the river only for a water supply. The canal was completed in 1825 and operated successfully for one hundred years, until it succumbed to the competition of the railroads.

Turning downstream at the tavern, the canal towpath leads eventually to Widewater, an ancient bed of the river which was dammed to serve as a portion of the canal. Earlier on the towpath, a turnoff leads over bridges to the overlook of the falls on Falls Island. Several hundred yards farther downstream on the canal, but well before Widewater, Billy Goat Trail leads from the towpath to the cliffs on the Maryland side of the gorge.

Billy Goat Trail is well-named, for in contrast to the relatively easy walk along the Virginia cliffs, this blue-blazed trail is a scramble. The spectacular potholes and rock sculpturing along this trail were caused by glacial erosion and the scouring action of sand-laden floodwaters.

As you would suspect, the gorge looks very different from a canoe or kayak. Many otherwise unnoticed details strike the eye when seen close up from water level. The stains on the rocks are caused by iron and manganese oxides. A three-foot-wide dark band, beginning several feet up from the stream at low water, is the result of the release of the oxides at high water from abandoned mines far up-stream. The stains occur principally on the rocks above eddies, where there is less scouring action from the swift current.

From a kayak, potholes and sculptured figures, gracefully layered patterns in the rocks, rib-rocked cliffs, grasses and phlox, and varicolored lichens compete for the eye's attention.

The Formation of the Falls and the Gorge

Before the Ice Age the Potomac River flowed in a broad, open valley over the hard rocks of the Piedmont Plateau and then down to the sea across the soft rocks of the Coastal Plain.

With the beginning of the Ice Age, two or three million years ago, water from the oceans formed thick sheets of ice on the land to the north. Sea level around the world fell as much as 500 feet. The lowered sea level caused the Potomac, probably swollen by melted snow, to cut deeply into the floor of its former valley. This down-cutting in the Piedmont, especially rapid where the hard rocks were broken by faults and closely spaced joints, produced the spectacular rocky gorge between Great Falls and Little Falls. At Great Falls the river encounters a series of thick hard ledges of ancient sandstone which are particularly resistant to erosion. These ledges support the falls and have slowed the progress of valley cutting. The present chutes through the falls follow the major zones of weakness, and the two-million-year-old process of carving continues.

Water Levels

The standard for measuring the level in this section of the river is a gauge near Little Falls and inside the Brookmont pumping station, which is seven miles downstream from the Great Falls. The reading of the level of the Potomac there and at other stations may be obtained by calling the U.S. Weather Service at 301-736-2500. The normal summer level of the river is three feet. At the height of the 1972 flood the gauge read more than twenty-two feet. In the flood of 1936 the gauge was at 28.6 feet.

The cutting power and force of the water is difficult to imagine. In the major floods of 1733, 1889, 1936, 1942, and 1972, the Potomac waters rose above what is now the ground-floor level in the Visitors Center on either side of the falls. In the main chute of the falls, a body of water 500 feet wide and eighty feet deep was moving at better than twenty miles per hour, laden with tons of sand, gravel, and boulders. During the flood of 1936, the water above Great Falls was only ten feet above drought level, but in Mather Gorge the water was eighty feet above normal. A similar relationship applies to the Little Falls gauge and Mather Gorge. An inch of change on the gauge may mean three to six or more inches in the gorge because it is a mere sixty feet wide at places.

The changes in the water levels are of great interest to boaters. By noting the state of the water in rapids at Rocky Islands, Wet Bottom Chute, and Difficult Run and then reading the Little Falls gauge on the same day, boaters learn to anticipate which rapids on a given day offer the most in white-water sport. The flow of water at three feet is 2500 cubic feet per second. At five feet it is ten times that. And at seven feet it is twenty times that at three feet. These flows are of vital interest to the residents of the Washington metropolitan area, since the river is the source of their drinking water.

From the shore, it is difficult to guess the depth of the river. Generally, the wider reaches of the river are shallow. Above and below the rapids, which are natural dams, the water is deeper. At Echo Cliffs the depth is about fifty feet; at the foot of Rocky Islands, about thirty.

The Photographs

The pictures which follow are divided into two sections, one on Great Falls and the other on the Gorge. The latter are in general arranged as though one were proceeding downstream to Difficult Run. The locations of the pictures are indicated on the map on the back of the book. The numbers on the map correspond to the page numbers of the pictures. The last two pictures were taken at Carderock, downstream and beyond the reach of the map. I could not resist them.

Great Falls
of the Potomac

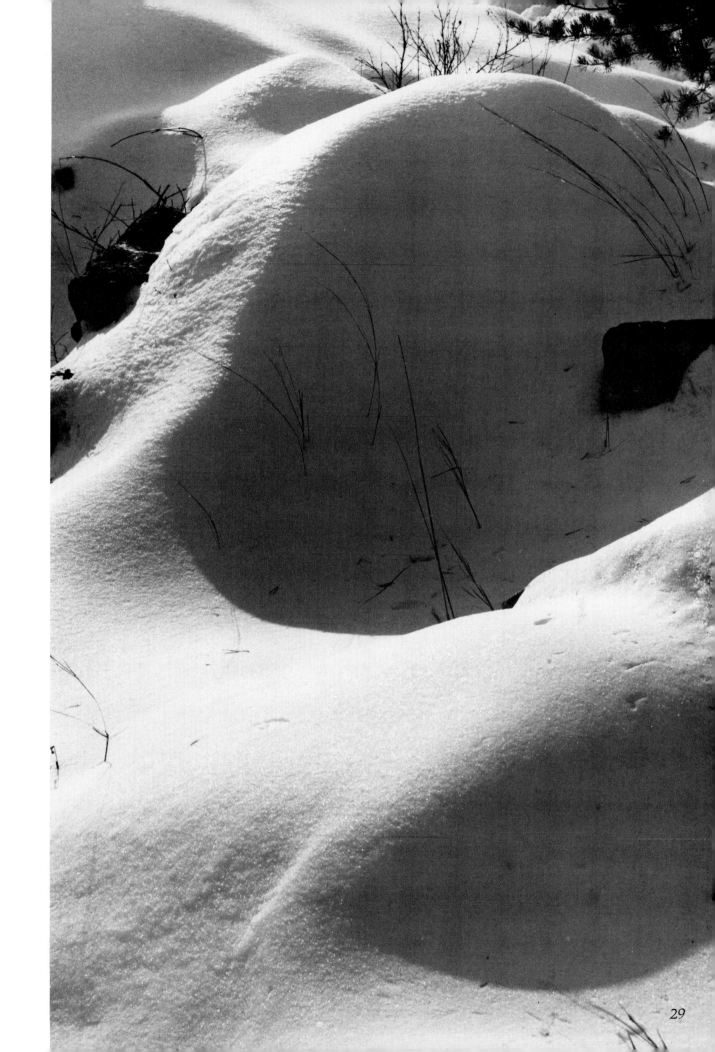

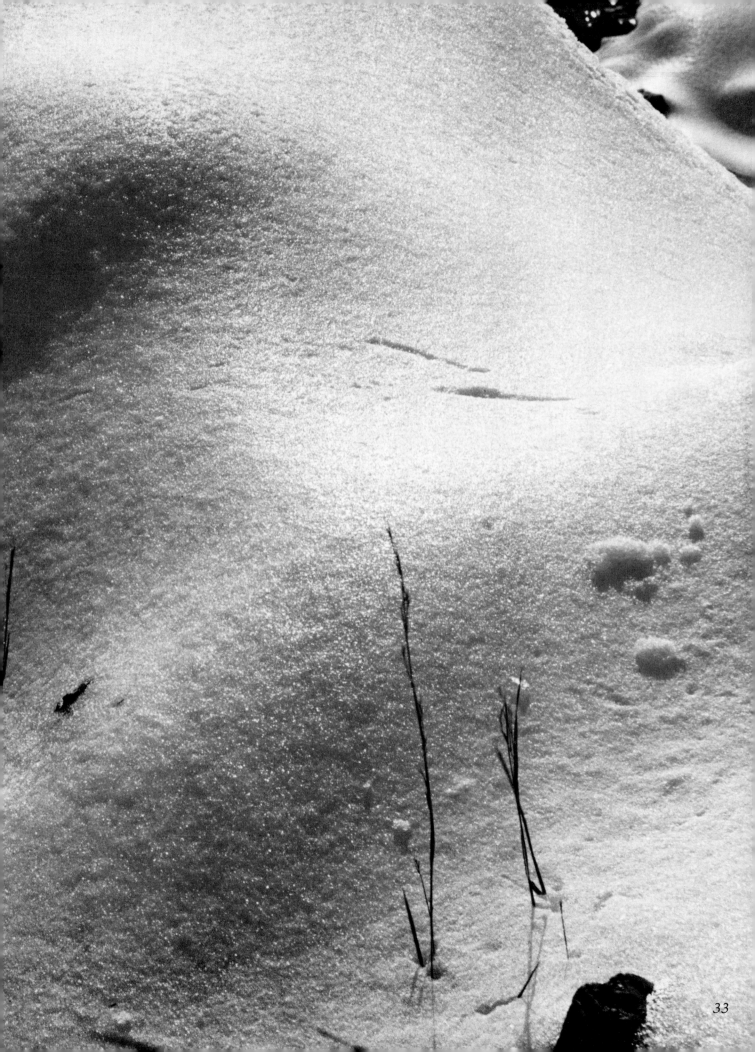

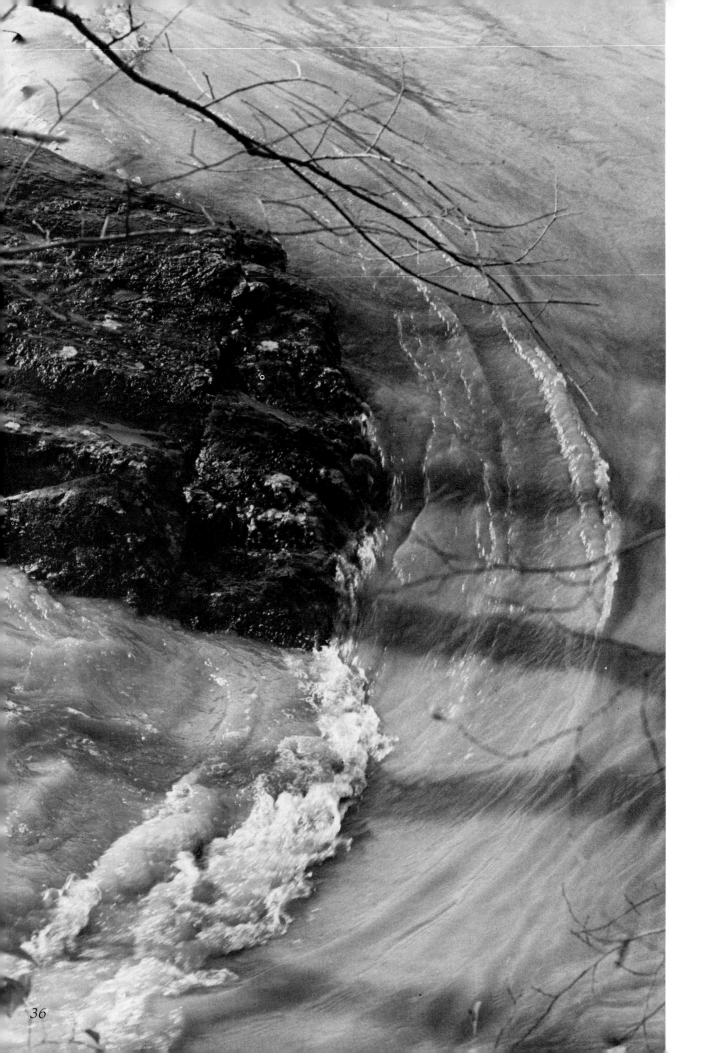

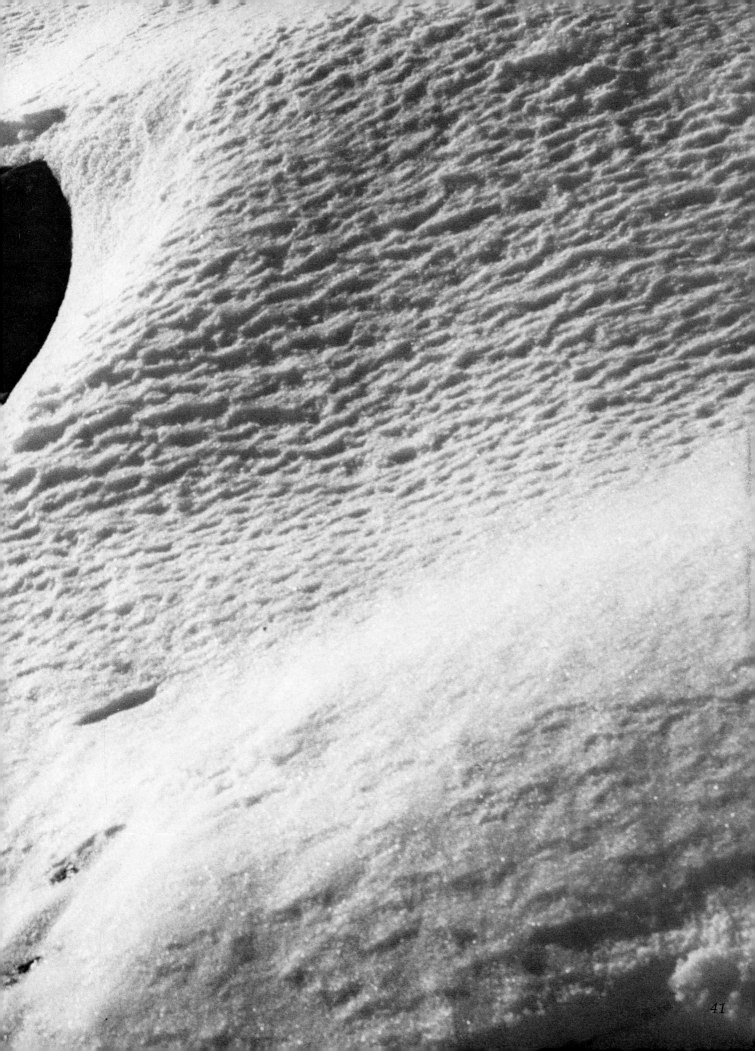

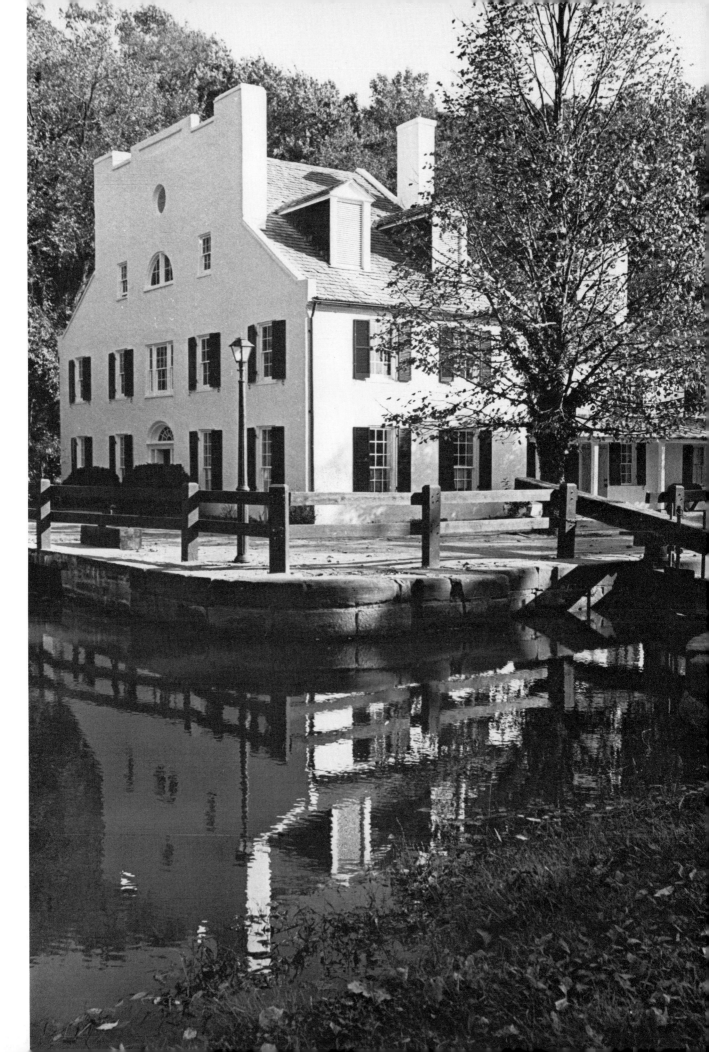

Mather Gorge

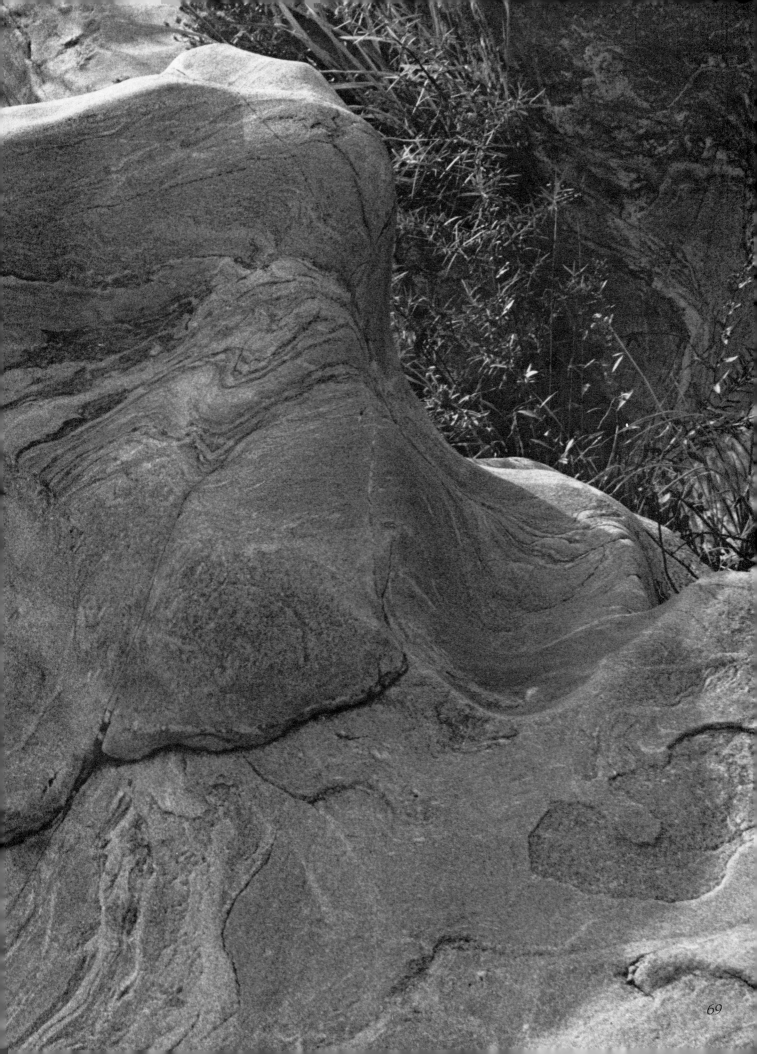

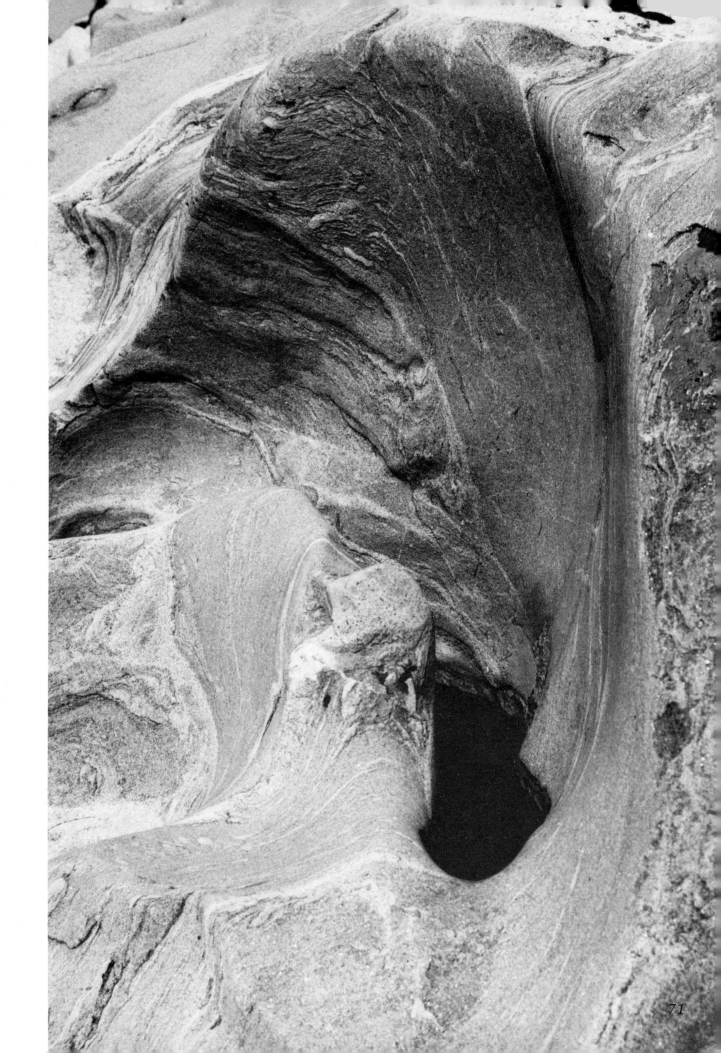

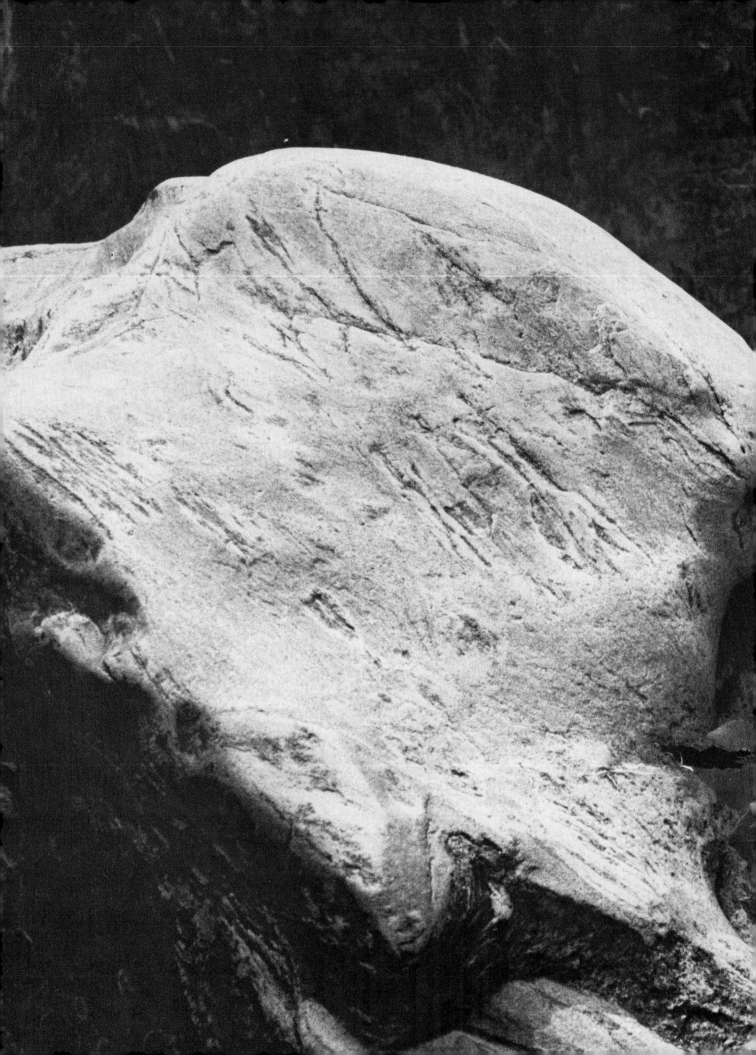

83

Photographic Notes

In photographing a river, a boat is a great convenience, and, in some cases, a necessity. Exploring points of view and gaining access to approaches would often be difficult or impossible without one. In the case of a river with strong currents and rapids, the kayak is the chosen craft because it is maneuverable and can be paddled upstream through the rapids.

In photographing the Potomac, although I did a lot of hiking, I relied principally on my kayak, carrying my cameras and lenses in a dry bag behind the seat. I stopped where I chose, to shoot from the shore, since a kayak is not a suitable platform for photography.

All the pictures in this book were taken with a handheld, 35-mm, single-lens reflex camera. The Exacta camera was used until old age overcame it several years ago. Then I changed to the Nikon FTN. About half the pictures were taken with each. The principal lenses used were the 35 mm and the 135 mm. The former lens provided a wide view with great depth of field. The latter allowed me to reach out and gain an intimate approach which the terrain would not have permitted with the 35-mm lens.

Although my preference in film for years had been Eastman's Panatomic-X because of the fine grain, I became dissatisfied with the slow speed of the film in marginal light conditions and when using the 135-mm lens. With the 135-mm lens I wanted to use a minimum speed of 1/250th of a second to eliminate body motion and also to shoot with a smaller aperture to achieve better depth of field.

Both of these needs could have been met by the use of a tripod, just as I might have achieved greater technical excellence with a view camera. But I did not like the idea of carrying the tripod about with me in the kayak, although it could have been done. For the same reasons, I have repeatedly rejected the 4 by 5 view camera. Also, the view camera is out of line with my darkroom and projection equipment, which is geared to 35-mm, as are all of my photographic habits.

My switch to Tri-X film was hastened by the comment of an Eastman representative several years ago, who told me that this film had the same grain quality as the Panatomic-X of ten years previous. Furthermore, a friend had suggested a development procedure which I find most satisfactory. It calls for development in Microdol-X diluted three to one at seventy-five degrees for 13½ minutes, which is 1½ minutes less than recommended by Eastman. The daylight tank is agitated vigorously for five seconds every minute instead of every thirty seconds. The result of this method is a less dense negative, tending to be normal or perhaps slightly on the flat side, occasionally requiring the use of a polycontrast filter #3.

Of course, development is related to the exposure. When using the Exacta, I didn't use a meter, but followed the instructions which come with the film. While this was quite satisfactory for normal light conditions, I lost my way in marginal ones. One result of using this method for over twenty-five years was that it forced me to study the light, which is, of course, what photography is all about. Experience quickly overcame my doubts about the Nikon FTN metering system. It is very reliable in a wide range of light conditions. The user is still required to think, to study the light, and to make certain allowances to achieve his objective.

Although I make contact sheets of the negatives for reference purposes, my routine procedure is to enlarge the full negative on eight by ten paper, which facilitates judgment of quality and interest. This routine discourages promiscuous shooting, since what is shot must be printed, and nothing is more boring in a darkroom than printing a bad negative.

I use Eastman's Polycontrast J double-weight paper exclusively, except where warm tones are desired. I feel it is important to stay with one camera, one film, and one paper as a means of ensuring greater mechanical and technical reliability. Then the mind is free for the purpose of photography, which is to see and photograph the subject. The reproductions for this book were made from photographs on Polycontrast J, and with few exceptions they are full negative. Since 35-mm color slides cannot be cropped, I early got the habit of composing the picture in the viewfinder rather than relying on later cropping in the darkroom.

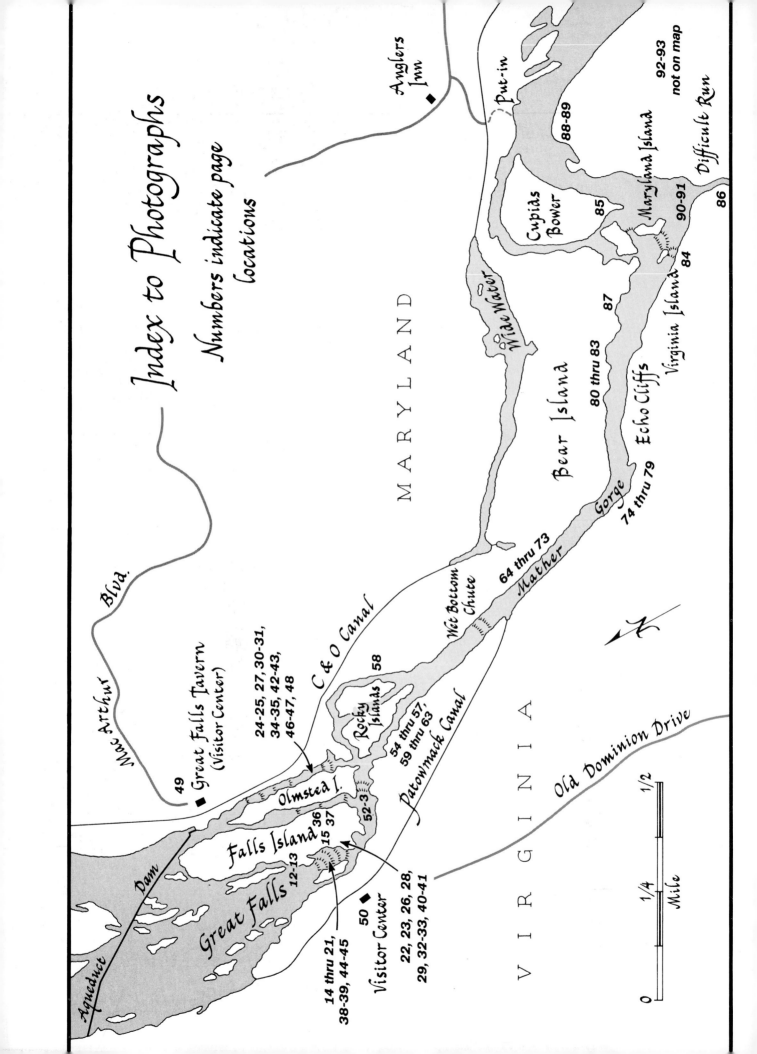

Index to Photographs

Numbers indicate page locations

Aqueduct

Dam

MacArthur Blvd.

49 ■ Great Falls Tavern (Visitor Center)

24-25, 27, 30-31, 34-35, 42-43, 46-47, 48

C & O Canal

MARYLAND

Olmsted I.

Falls Island   36
             15 37

Great Falls 12-13

14 thru 21, 38-39, 44-45

50 ■ Visitor Center

22, 23, 26, 28, 29, 32-33, 40-41

52-3

Rocky Islands   58

54 thru 57, 59 thru 63

Patowmack Canal

Wet Bottom Chute

64 thru 73

Mather

Bear Island

80 thru 83

Gorge

74 thru 79

Echo Cliffs

Virginia Island   84

Wide Water

Cupids Bower

85

87

90-91   Maryland Island

86   Difficult Run

88-89

Put-in

92-93 not on map

■ Anglers Inn

VIRGINIA

Old Dominion Drive

N

0   1/4   1/2
        Mile